AMERICA AT WAR
KOREAN WAR

JOHN PERRITANO

Library of Congress Cataloging-in-Publication Data

Perritano, John.

Korean War / [John Perritano].

p. cm. — (America at war)

Includes index.

ISBN 0-531-24910-7/978-0-531-24910-9 (pbk.)
1. Korean War, 1950-1953--Juvenile literature.
2. Korean War, 1950-1953—United States—Juvenile
literature. I. Title.

DS918.P44 2010

951.904'2—dc22

2010035048

This edition published by
Scholastic Inc., 557 Broadway; New York, NY

SCHOLASTIC, FRANKLIN WATTS, and associated logos are
trademarks and/or registered trademarks of Scholastic Inc.

232751 10/10

Printed in Heshan City, China
10 9 8 7 6 5 4 3 2 1

Created by Q2AMedia
www.q2amedia.com

Text, design & illustrations Copyright © Q2AMedia 2011

Editor Jessica Cohn   **Designer** Neha Kaul & Isha Khanna
Publishing Director Chester Fisher   **Project Manager** Kunal Mehrotra
Client Service Manager Santosh Vasudevan   **Art Editor** Sujatha Menon
Art Director Joita Das   **Picture Researcher** Debobrata Sen
Senior Designer Ritu Chopra

CONTENTS

Morning Calm	4
Global Struggle	6
Invasion	8
Breach of Peace	10
Pusan	12
Inchon	14
Into the North	16
China Enters the War	18
Chosin	20
Weapons of War	22
Truman and MacArthur	24
A New General	26
Searching for Peace	28
Aftermath	30
Index	32

MORNING CALM

President Harry S. Truman did not like Washington, D.C. "If you want a friend in Washington, get a dog," he said. His wife, Bess, did not care for Washington, either. She spent most of her time at their home in Independence, Missouri.

The Trumans were in Missouri on June 24, 1950. The president and his family were enjoying a warm summer weekend. Far away, in Korea, war was breaking out. Korea was known as the "Land of the Morning Calm." But it was far from calm there. A U.S. newspaper reporter was in Seoul, the capital of South Korea. He was the first to report that North Korean soldiers had invaded South Korea.

South Korean President Syngman Rhee (right) greets U.S. General Douglas MacArthur.

World War III

The attacks began in Korea on June 25. Dean Acheson was the U.S. secretary of state. He phoned to tell the president the bad news. Truman was concerned. He knew that a war in Korea could result in an even wider conflict. That fighting might snowball into a third world war. He immediately left Missouri. Truman returned to Washington to deal with the problem. The Korean War became the first armed showdown of the **Cold War** era.

History of a Nation Divided

Korea was once one country. The Koreans traded goods with the Chinese. Korea copied Chinese buildings, religion, and government.

Japan ruled Korea during World War II (1939–1945). After the war, the United States and Soviet Union split Korea into two countries. They used the 38th **parallel** as a dividing line. North Korea was led by Kim Il-sung. South Korea was run by Syngman Rhee. The North was run by the Workers Party of North Korea. They believed in **communism**.

Major Warring Nations:

China
North Korea
South Korea
United States and its **United Nations** Allies
Leaders:
  China: Mao Zedong
  South Korea: Syngman Rhee
  North Korea: Kim Il-sung
  United States: Harry S. Truman
Top Generals:
  Douglas MacArthur: United States
  Matthew Ridgeway: United States

CHINA

U.S.S.R.

Hyesan

Kanggye

Sinuiju

Iwon

Korea Bay

NORTH KOREA

P'yongyang

Wonsan

East Sea
(Sea of Japan)

Haeju

Kaesong

38th Parallel

Seoul

SOUTH KOREA

Yellow Sea

Andong

Kunsan

P'ohang

Daegu

Mokp'o

Masan

Pusan

JAPAN

Korea in 1950

Cold War—a fight of ideas between communism and the Western democracies, which began after World War II (WWII)

parallel—imaginary line of latitude; distance from Earth's equator to its poles

communism—government in which individuals do not own property

United Nations—world organization formed after WWII to promote peace

GLOBAL STRUGGLE

| The United States was the champion of Western *democracies* during the Cold War. The Soviets led the communist nations.

The U.S. and the Soviet Union had been **allies** in World War II. But they became enemies after the war. In 1948, they had a standoff in Berlin, Germany. The city of Berlin was divided after WWII. West Berlin was being run by democratic nations. The Soviets did not like the setup. They tried to stop food and supplies from reaching West Berlin. But the U.S. flew in the goods that were needed. The two countries did not battle with guns in Berlin. Instead, they fought with their actions. They continued this kind of fighting throughout the Cold War. Each nation formed **alliances** to try to gain power.

Containment

U.S. officials did not want communism to spread. The U.S. built military bases near the Soviet Union. It was a way to try to stop the Soviets from taking over other countries. That plan was known as "containment." Some of those bases were in South Korea.

Chinese leader Chiang Kai-shek, who was replaced by Mao Zedong.

China

Soon, the Cold War was being fought in the Far East. After WWII, China was run by the Nationalist Chinese. In 1949, communists took over. They were led by Mao Zedong. The Nationalists moved to the island of Formosa (Taiwan). Mao signed a **treaty** with the Soviets. Many people thought Truman had "lost" China to communism. He was blamed for not giving enough help to the Nationalists.

Soviet leader Joseph Stalin (left) and U.S. President Harry Truman (right)

Grave Threat

At the start of the Cold War, only the U.S. had atomic weapons. That changed in 1949. That year the Soviets were successful in making an atomic bomb. Many people feared that the communists were ready to challenge the United States in Asia. U.S. leaders did not think Korea would become a battleground, however. During that time, the U.S. was bringing troops back from Korea. Various U.S. officials even said that the U.S. would not help if South Koreans were attacked.

democracies—governments in which the people have power
allies—groups and individuals joined to help one another
alliances—partnerships
treaty—an agreement

INVASION

In Korea, life was hard on both sides. Some families were actually torn apart when the country was cut in two. Most people lived in the South, which grew most of the rice. Most raw materials, such as coal and wood, were produced in the North.

Soon, U.N. tanks would rumble through Seoul, the capital of South Korea. ▼

The United Nations (U.N.) wanted to unite Korea. The Soviets refused. South Korea turned to the United States for help. North Korea looked to the Soviet Union for aid. They got help from the People's Republic of China, too. Fear between the North and South ran high. Soldiers from both sides made military raids across the border. South Koreans did not want to live under a communist **dictator**. But the North had a stronger army. It was supplied by the Soviets. It was strengthened by Korean-born, battle-tested warriors. Many of them had served in Mao's army in China.

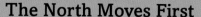

The North Moves First

In the summer of 1950, Kim Il-sung decided to unite North and South by force. He asked the Soviets for permission. On June 25, the North crossed the 38th parallel. North Korea's **artillery** shot at the South. About 100,000 North Korean troops and 150 Soviet tanks then moved southward. "North Korean forces invaded the Republic of Korea at several places this morning," U.S. Ambassador John J. Muccio wrote to the State Department, "It would appear from the nature of the attack [that this is] an all-out **offensive** against the Republic of Korea."

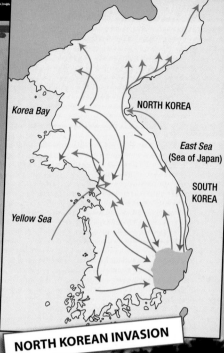

NORTH KOREAN INVASION

The red arrows show the North's movements from June to November in 1950. The blue arrows show the U.N.

dictator—leader who rules with absolute power
artillery—large moveable guns, such as rockets and cannons
offensive—an attack

BREACH OF PEACE

The attack was a complete surprise. The communists poured into the South, ready to take over. They moved deep into the heart of South Korea.

The South Korean army retreated in a panic. By June 28th, the North had captured Seoul. That is the South's capital. They then pushed farther south. This left the South Korean army in trouble. The South Koreans could not defend their country, and their army limped southward.

Refugees head south in Korea in 1951. ▼

U.N. Responds

Truman asked the United Nations for help. The U.N. ordered the North Koreans to stop the invasion. They refused. President Truman believed that this was a threat to Western democracies. He **mobilized** the U.S. military and urged the United Nations to send troops. More than a dozen nations—including the U.S.—decided to send troops to help the South. They would fight under the flag of the U.N.

Harry S. Truman stands over Dean Acheson, as he signs a treaty.

MacArthur in Charge

The U.N. was responsible for defending South Korea. But the U.S. took the lead. Truman believed the attack was "inspired" by the Soviet Union. "If we don't put up a fight now," he said to his staff, there was "no telling what they'll do." He placed General Douglas MacArthur in charge of the U.N. forces.

mobilized—assembled and made ready for war

PUSAN

Soldiers who had served in World War II were asked to fight again. The U.S. government also *drafted* new *recruits*.

By early July, the North was moving across Korea. But standing between them and victory was a U.S. general. His name was Walton H. "Bulldog" Walker. On July 2, the first U.S. troops arrived from bases in Japan, and General Walker took command. At first, the North Koreans were able to push Walker and his troops back to Pusan. That is a port on the Sea of Japan. At Pusan, however, Walker and the U.S. Eighth Army fought a historic battle.

U.S. troops fire across the Naktong River. ▼

CHINA

NORTH KOREA

Korea Bay

East Sea
(Sea of Japan)

● Kangwon-do
● Seoul

West Sea
(Yellow Sea)

SOUTH KOREA

Pusan Perimeter

● PUSAN

South Sea
(East China Sea)

PUSAN BATTLE

The green shows the area the U.N. troops defended. The red arrows show the North's attack.

No Retreat

The U.S. troops had their backs to the sea and nowhere to run. The battle-tested Walker told his men: "We are fighting a battle against time. There will be no more **retreating** [or] **withdrawal** . . . There is no line behind us to which we can retreat."

Standing Tall

Walker and his army had a bloody struggle with the North Koreans. It lasted six weeks. Walker's army used the Naktong River to block the enemy. The North's army punished the American lines with wave after wave of attacks. But Walker's men stood their ground. Walker oversaw the entire battle. He traveled from outpost to outpost by plane or jeep. He directed his men to move from one position to another. Walker's defense of Pusan gave the United Nations time to send more troops.

drafted—forced into military service
recruits—new soldiers or sailors
retreating—moving backward
withdrawal—act of leaving a place

INCHON

In the United States, General Douglas MacArthur was considered a war hero. He had led U.S. forces to victory over Japan in World War II.

MacArthur was a famous. He was also self-important. He considered himself a military genius. Once in command of U.N. forces, he made big plans. He did what many historians say was one of the smartest moves in military history.

He attacked from behind enemy lines. MacArthur's goal was to destroy supply lines. He also wanted to crush the North between his troops and those of General Walker in Pusan.

Marines come ashore at Inchon. ▼

General Douglas MacArthur

Daring Attack

MacArthur chose the most unlikely place to launch his attack—the port city of Inchon.

Inchon is on North Korea's upper west coast. The entrance to Inchon's harbor is narrow. It was protected by huge guns on the shore. What made an attack at Inchon especially dangerous, however, was its tide. Inchon has one of the highest tides in the world. It rises more than 30 feet before quickly falling. The ships carrying American troops had to land at high tide at just the right time.

Success

MacArthur's bosses in Washington were the **Joint Chiefs of Staff.** They did not like the plan at first, but he won them over. The invasion began just before dawn on September 15, 1950. First, the Navy bombed the shore. At high tide, Americans entered the harbor's channel. The attack caught the North Koreans by surprise. MacArthur's troops quickly captured Inchon. They recaptured Seoul soon after.

Walker's troops pushed out of Pusan at the same time. They then chased the North Koreans north across the 38th parallel. U.N. forces took more than 100,000 North Korean soldiers prisoner. The North's army nearly disappeared from the South. Victory for the U.N. seemed near, or so many people thought.

Joint Chiefs of Staff—group of military leaders who advise the president on military matters

INTO THE NORTH

Truman believed that the farther north the U.N. pushed, the more likely it was that there would be trouble. He feared that the Chinese or Russians would join the side of the North Koreans. The president feared the use of nuclear weapons.

MacArthur's goal was to conquer the North. The Joint Chiefs of Staff told the general he could do battle north of the 38th parallel. However, the Joint Chiefs ordered him not to cross the border into China or the Soviet Union.

U.N. troops crossed the 38th parallel on October 1. They captured P'yongyang, the capital of North Korea. MacArthur's troops inched closer to the Yalu River. That is the waterway separating China from North Korea. Truman and his aides grew uneasy. Truman ordered MacArthur to keep American forces away from the Yalu. China had warned several times that it would not allow troops near the border.

Wake Island

Truman ordered MacArthur to meet him on Wake Island in the Pacific Ocean. They met on October 15. The general told the president that the Chinese would not fight. He claimed that the war would be over by Thanksgiving. MacArthur also said that if the Chinese did enter the war, U.N. troops would "slaughter" them. He would soon be proven wrong.

U.N. forces cross
▼ *the 38th parallel.*

CHINA ENTERS THE WAR

U.N. troops were in position near the Chinese-North Korean border. They heard bugles begin to blow. Many were scared by the sound. Then, the Chinese arrived, in wave after human wave.

For months the Chinese had secretly gathered troops along the border. Small groups of Chinese "volunteers" began battling U.N. troops in October 1950. A huge attack began in early November. About 30,000 well-equipped and well-trained Chinese soldiers crossed into North Korea. They were screaming and blowing bugles. The might of the troops left the Americans and their allies in a panic.

▲ Chinese soldiers stand ready for orders.

Every Man for Himself

"It was every man for himself," one American soldier said. "The shooting was terrific, there were Chinese shouting everywhere. I didn't know which way to go. In the end, I just ran with the crowd." The addition of Chinese troops changed the tide of battle. The Chinese pulled back after that first attack. But they soon came back.

New War

MacArthur decided to launch a huge offensive at the end of November. His troops were ordered to the Yalu River. He declared that the attack would win the war and "bring the boys back home before Christmas." It was a terrible mistake. More than 200,000 Chinese troops streamed across the river at the start of the offensive. MacArthur was shaken. " We face an entirely new war," he said.

The Chinese quickly took prisoners. These U.N. soldiers were among those captured as fighting continued.

CHOSIN

Some of the roughest fighting during the Chinese attack happened near the Chosin *Reservoir*, near the Yalu River.

General Edward M. "Ned" Almond was the commander of the U.N forces in the area. MacArthur told Almond to push to the Yalu. But the Chinese had other plans. They were like no enemy the Americans had ever met before. The Chinese troops were well trained. They carried very little equipment. During the day, Chinese scouts looked for the best paths to follow. At night, Chinese soldiers followed those trails. They moved swiftly and quietly before attacking.

Marines battle at Chosin, November 27, 1950.

"That's Impossible"

U.N. troops—mostly American—took up their positions at Chosin on November 27. More than 120,000 Chinese troops marched to meet them. The Chinese killed many U.N. soldiers before those troops had a chance to fight back. "That's impossible," Almond yelled when told of the attack. Almond did not believe that there were that many Chinese troops in North Korea. "We're still attacking and going all the way to the Yalu," he told his officers.

"Chosin Few"

The Chinese quickly broke through the U.N. lines in several places. The U.N. troops were forced to run. The 1st Marine Division was surrounded at Chosin. The Chinese blasted the U.S. soldiers and Marines. The weather was cold and snowy. Many of the U.S. weapons were useless in the below-zero temperatures. Thousands died in hand-to-hand combat. Yet, some Marines who fought there lived to tell about it. They became known as the "Chosin Few." They fought hard. They battled their way out.

reservoir—place where water collects

WEAPONS OF WAR

In Korea, helicopters and jet fighters were used in ways that shaped how America fought in future wars.

Helicopters were workhorses in Korea. The United Nations used "choppers" to remove wounded soldiers from the battlefield. Pilots flew helicopters to rescue downed pilots from behind enemy lines. The U.S. Navy used helicopters during rescue operations. The Marines used a special type of helicopter to move troops to battle zones.

A U.S. helicopter takes part in an invasion on ▼ *September 20, 1951.*

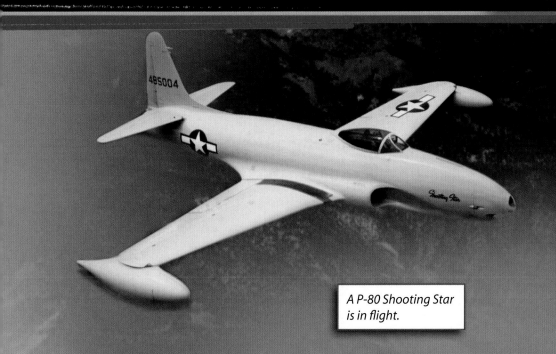

A P-80 Shooting Star is in flight.

Jet Fighters

Britain, the United States, and Germany had airplanes powered by jet engines during World War II. At the time, the **technology** was new. Not many of the jets saw action. The Korean War was the first war where jet fighters showed their worth. Chinese and North Korean pilots flew jets called MiGs. The MiGs were supplied by the Soviets. Americans had a jet fighter called the Lockheed P-80 Shooting Star. On November 8, 1950, a Shooting Star flown by Lieutenant Russell Brown destroyed a MiG. It was the first all-jet air battle in history.

U.S. pilots also flew a fighter called the U.S. Skynight. It had twin engines. It carried **radar**, which allowed it to fight at night.

Napalm

During World War II, napalm was the main ingredient in flamethrowers. The gel-like chemical would stick to whatever it was sprayed on. That included tanks, trees, and soldiers. It would then burst into flames. U.S. forces used much more napalm during the Korean War, however. The U.S. dropped a quarter of a million pounds of napalm bombs from airplanes each day.

technology—science that builds machines and other things that work in the world
radar—system that uses radio waves to "see" objects

TRUMAN AND MACARTHUR

By the beginning of 1951, the U.N. was on the run. "This is a sight that hasn't been seen for hundreds of years," one officer said, "the men of the whole United States Army fleeing from the battlefield."

The war was not going well. MacArthur said that the only way to win was to bomb military bases in China. He also wanted the U.S. Navy to create a **blockade**. This would cut China off from the rest of the world. Truman studied the plan and told MacArthur no. Truman did not want to start World War III. The Soviet Union might strike in Western Europe if bombs fell on China.

President Truman meets General MacArthur on Wake Island.

Different Views

MacArthur thought Truman was making a mistake. He protested Truman's decision. He complained to people. They included members of Congress, who told the public about the general's views. Truman was angry. Some officials told the general he was wrong to talk that way about the president. Still, MacArthur continued to press his plan. In March 1951, MacArthur asked for permission to use the atomic bomb against China.

...red!

...uman had finally had enough
...his **insubordinate** general.
...esident Truman was General
...cArthur's boss. It was
...cArthur's duty to obey the
...sident's orders. Truman
...ided that MacArthur could
...onger lead the troops. The
...sident removed the general
...n his post on April 11, 1951.

The standoff between the president and the general was big news in 1951.

...o's Welcome

...Arthur's firing set off a storm of protests
...e United States. MacArthur had not been
...e in 15 years. When he returned, he was given
...o's welcome. The president, however, stuck to
...ecision. Years later, historians tend to agree that
...MacArthur was the right thing for Truman to do.

blockade—a military action to stop people or goods from entering or leaving
insubordinate—disobedient

A NEW GENERAL

Truman tapped General Matthew Ridgeway to replace MacArthur. General "Bullog" Walker had died in a jeep accident after fighting at Pusan. Ridgeway had taken his place. Ridgeway was an "army brat." He had grown up on military bases. Ridgeway once wrote that his earliest memories were of "guns" and "marching men."

U.N. troops fight in the streets of Seoul. ▼

Truman congratulates General Matthew Ridgeway at West Point.

Ridgeway had served in World War II. He was now responsible for turning defeat into victory. He had proved himself during the long, cold winter of 1950–1951. That was when U.N. troops were retreating southward. Ridgeway had taken over the Eighth Army. He had stopped the U.N. retreat below Seoul. The army had regrouped. Then, they had marched northward again. Under Ridgeway, the U.N. was able to take back Seoul. U.N. troops were again at the 38th parallel in March 1951.

Ridgeway took command of the U.N. forces in April. At the same time, the North Koreans launched one last offensive to win the war. The U.N. beat back the charge. On June 23, 1951, the Soviet Union's representative at the United Nations proposed peace talks.

SEARCHING FOR PEACE

Peace talks began on July 10, 1951. They took place in a tiny village near the 38th parallel.

The talks lasted two years. Fighting continued during the talks. The war dragged on. The Chinese dug tunnels into the mountains. They used these as command centers. The tunnels protected them during U.N. air strikes. Even so, neither side was winning. Both sides battled bad weather during the summer and winter. The war went nowhere fast.

◀ *Delegates sign the agreement, with representatives of the U.N. to the left and North Korea to the right.*

POWs

At the center of the peace talks were the fates of prisoners of war, or POWs. The United Nations charged that the communists beat, starved, and **brainwashed** their prisoners. The Chinese and North Koreans said that prisoners caught by South Korea were shot and beaten.

Each side wanted its POWs returned. But the U.N. wanted to give prisoners a chance to stay in the South if they wanted it. The communists finally agreed to allow POWs to stay in U.N. camps for three months. The POWs had to decide where to go after their stay.

More Territory

Both sides continued to do damage as the peace talks dragged on. China and North Korea tried to capture as much land as possible. The U.S. destroyed dams. These were the structures that provided North Korea with water for farming. China and North Korea charged the U.N. with using **germ warfare**. At last, they reached an agreement. The U.N., North Korea, and China signed an **armistice** on July 27, 1953. The agreement established a 150-mile **demilitarized zone**. Neither side could cross it. Korea was still not one country, but the fighting ended.

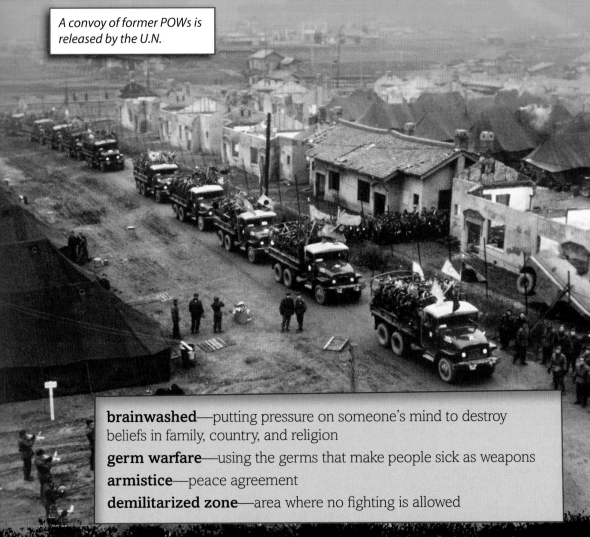

A convoy of former POWs is released by the U.N.

brainwashed—putting pressure on someone's mind to destroy beliefs in family, country, and religion

germ warfare—using the germs that make people sick as weapons

armistice—peace agreement

demilitarized zone—area where no fighting is allowed

AFTERMATH

The war had killed or wounded about three million Koreans. Most of them were regular citizens, not troops. More than five million Koreans became **refugees** without homes. The Chinese lost one million people. About 33,700 U.S. troops died.

The war destroyed much of the nations' businesses and farms. South Korea's economy made gains in the years that followed. North Korea, however, cut itself off from the world. Neither side traded with each other. Families that were separated remained apart. In the 1990s, a **famine** killed more than two million North Koreans. In October 2006, North Korea became a **nuclear power**. Several attempts to unite North and South have failed. Both sides accepted a cease-fire. But no treaty was signed. They are still in a state of war.

Barbed wire marks the demilitarized zone.

Korean War Time Line

June 25, 1950
North Korea invades South Korea

June 27, 1950
President Harry S. Truman orders General Douglas MacArthur to send ammunition and equipment to Seoul, South Korea

June 28, 1950
North Korean soldiers enter Seoul

June 30, 1950
MacArthur receives permission to send U.S. ground forces to the Korean peninsula

July 2, 1950
The first U.S. forces arrive in Korea

September 15, 1950
U.N. forces invade Inchon

September 26-30, 1950
U.S. forces fight for and recapture Seoul

October 15, 1950
Truman meets MacArthur at Wake Island

October 25, 1950
U.S. troops capture Chinese "volunteer" soldiers near the Chosin Reservoir

November 26, 1950
The U.N. faces huge Chinese forces

April 11, 1951
Truman fires MacArthur

July 10, 1951
Truce talks begin

July 27, 1953
U.N., China, and North Korea sign a cease-fire agreement

The Forgotten War

The Korean War is sometimes called the "Forgotten War." That is in part because it did not have a clear winner as other wars did. Those who fought in Korea, however, can never forget. They still have memories of battle. They fought at Chosin, Pusan, Inchon, and elsewhere. U.S. forces are still in South Korea, protecting the country.

▲ *Seoul, capital of South Korea*

▲ *P'yongyang, capital of North Korea*

refugees—people who must run away from their homes

famine—shortage of food

nuclear power—country that has learned how to use the power of the atom

INDEX

38th parallel 5, 9, 16, 17, 27, 28

Acheson, Dean 4, 11

Almond, Edward M. 20, 21

Brown, Russell 23

Chosin 20, 21, 31

communism 5, 7

demilitarized zone 29

Il-sung, Kim 5, 9

Inchon 14, 15, 31

Joint Chiefs of Staff 15, 16

Lockheed P-80 23

MacArthur, Douglas 5, 11, 14, 15,
    19, 24, 25, 31

MiG 23

Muccio, John J. 9

napalm 23

Pusan 12-14, 31

P'yongyang 16

Rhee, Syngman 5

Ridgeway, Matthew 26, 27

Seoul 10, 15, 27

Truman, Harry S. 4, 5, 7, 11, 16,
    24-26, 31

Walker, Walton H. 12-15

United Nations (U.N.) 8, 9, 11,
    13-21, 24, 26-29, 31

Wake Island 16

Zedong, Mao 5-8